Bruce Lee

Greg Roensch
AR B.L.: 7.9 Alt.: 1184
Points: 1.0   UG

Martial Arts Masters

Bruce Lee

Greg Roensch

The Rosen Publishing Group, Inc.
New York

Published in 2002 by The Rosen Publishing Group, Inc.
29 East 21st Street, New York, NY 10010

First Edition

Library of Congress Cataloging-in-Publication Data

Roensch, Greg.
Bruce Lee / by Greg Roensch.— 1st ed.
p. cm. — (Martial arts masters)
Filmography: p.
Includes bibliographical references and index. Summary: A biography of the well-known actor and martial arts master, Bruce Lee, from his childhood in Hong Kong to his untimely death at the age of thirty-two.
ISBN 0-8239-3515-9 (lib. bdg.)
1. Lee, Bruce, 1940–1973—Juvenile literature. 2. Actors—United States—Biography—Juvenile literature. [1. Lee, Bruce, 1940–1973. 2. Actors and actresses. 3. Martial artists.] I. Title. II. Series.
PN2287.L2897 .R64 2002
791.43'028'092—dc21

                                          2001004720

Manufactured in the United States of America

Table of Contents

Despite a career cut short by his sudden death when he wa
only thirty-two years old, Bruce Lee became a world-famous
martial arts legend.

During his short life, Bruce Lee became the most famous martial artist and the biggest martial arts movie star the world had ever seen. Before Jackie Chan or Chuck Norris or Jean-Claude Van Damme, there was Bruce Lee.

Bruce Lee was only thirty-two years old when he died unexpectedly in 1973. Even though he became very famous in the last years of his life, this was nothing compared to the fame he gained after his death. Unfortunately, Lee did not live to enjoy his greatest movie triumph. *Enter the Dragon*, still regarded by many as the best martial arts movie of all time, was released a few weeks after his death. Still, the fact remains that Bruce Lee's short life had a tremendous impact on action movies and on the martial arts, and his influence continues to this day.

The martial arts have come a long way since the time when Lee was making movies and teaching martial arts. Today there are martial arts schools everywhere. And you can see martial arts in all sorts of movies and television shows today. Think of *Teenage Mutant Ninja Turtles*; *The Karate Kid*; *Walker, Texas Ranger*; and so many other examples. This wasn't

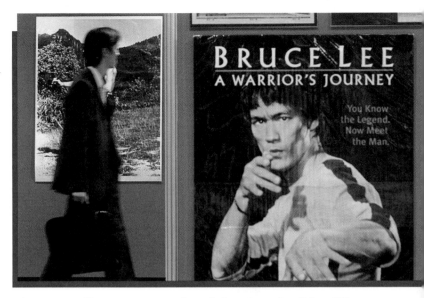

A man walks past artwork celebrating the life of Bruce Lee at the Dragon Expo 2000 in Hong Kong on November 27, 2000. It would have been Lee's sixtieth birthday.

the case when Bruce Lee started his career. When he jumped high in the air and kicked his opponents, it was as if his moves exploded off the screen. It was something very new and exciting for American audiences. With an equally explosive personality, Lee opened the door for the martial arts boom

Before Bruce Lee, Hollywood films featuring an Asian part—even in the lead role—were typically cast with non-Asian actors.

we see in society and in the entertainment industry today.

But it wasn't easy for Bruce Lee to bring a groundbreaking brand of action to the big screen. As an actor, he had to overcome racial prejudice and stereotypes in the Hollywood film industry. In those days, there were hardly any roles for Asian actors in American movies or television shows. If there was a part for an Asian actor, it was usually a very minor one and usually something less than favorable, such as a servant. On the whole, industry executives in Hollywood could not imagine an Asian actor as a major movie star in the United States. Bruce Lee struggled against this kind of prejudice throughout his career, but he eventually proved to the entire world that an Asian actor could become a true force at the box office. His success paved the way for actors like Jackie Chan, Chow Yun Fat, Jet Li, and Michelle Yeoh to become major Hollywood and international superstars.

Bruce Lee became a movie star in America against all odds. But that wasn't all he did. More important to him, Lee was a martial arts pioneer. He worked very hard to perfect his martial arts skills. By studying all sorts of different martial arts, he improved his skills by mixing the best techniques of other styles into his art. He was also a dynamic and inspirational martial arts teacher, and he viewed his movies as a way of teaching the martial arts to a whole new audience. Eventually, Lee created his own martial art, which he called jeet kune do.

It wasn't easy being a martial arts pioneer in the United States. In Hollywood, Lee had to combat prejudice in order to become an actor, and he also faced racial barriers as a martial artist. In the martial arts world, Lee had to struggle against the traditional martial arts masters who didn't want their fighting arts taught to non-Asians. Lee fought hard to overcome such obstacles, and now, several decades after his death, his influence in the martial arts is stronger than ever.

One of Bruce Lee's most famous techniques was the "one-inch punch." At a martial arts demonstration in 1964, Lee stood face-to-face against another martial artist. With his fist placed only one inch away from his opponent's chest, Lee unleashed so much power that his opponent was knocked off his feet. The audience was stunned that this small man could generate so much power.

Looking back, it seems like Bruce Lee's short life had the same kind of impact as that famous one-inch punch. The punch happened so quickly, you could only marvel at its explosive power. It was the same with Lee's life. Over so quickly, but containing such incredible power, Bruce Lee's life had an impact like nothing seen before or since.

Chapter 1

Birth of the Dragon

Bruce Lee was born at the Jackson Street Hospital in San Francisco's Chinatown district on November 27, 1940. From the instant of his birth, Lee was destined to be a dragon. Not only was he born in the Chinese year of the dragon, but he was also born in the hour of the dragon (between 6 AM and 8 AM). According to Chinese belief, the dragon is a symbol of extraordinary power and good luck. The date and time of Lee's birth was an omen that he was meant to reach the highest goals. Later in life, Lee would fulfill his destiny by starring in films such as *Enter the Dragon* and becoming an international superstar and martial arts pioneer.

Bruce Lee's father was Lee Hoi Chuen, a popular actor in Hong Kong. Lee Hoi Chuen and his wife, Grace, were traveling to the United States with a Chinese opera company when Lee, the little dragon, was born. Lee's parents gave him the Chinese name of Lee Jun Fan, which in English means "return again." Note that in Chinese culture, the family name comes first. They named Lee "return again" because they had a feeling their son would one day return to the United States. One of the nurses at the hospital gave him the English name Bruce.

Because his father was an actor, Lee spent much of his childhood around the stage and screen. In fact, his first screen appearance occurred when he was only three months old. In a movie called *The Golden Gate Girl*, Lee's father carried the young boy in his first role, in which he played the part of a baby girl. Lee would become very familiar with the sights and sounds of the moviemaking world. Though he never had formal training as an actor when he was growing up, Lee learned how to act by watching other actors. Born into an actor's family, it was as if this dragon was destined to be an actor.

Growing Up in Hong Kong

In 1941, Bruce Lee's family returned to Hong Kong, where Lee's father continued his career as an actor. At one time, Lee's father even worked as a supporting actor in a series of martial arts films. Martial arts movies have been popular in Asia for many years, but they wouldn't become popular in the United States until much later— not until Bruce Lee became a martial arts movie star.

As Lee grew up, he often accompanied his father to work and got much exposure to the world of moviemaking. Eventually, he was noticed by directors and given roles. When he was six years old, Bruce had a part in a movie called *The Beginning of a Boy*. During Lee's

A bustling street corner in Hong Kong in 1949. Bruce Lee grew up in this Chinese city, and left for the United States when he was nineteen years old.

Hong Kong acting career, his stage name became Lee Siu Lung, which means "Lee Little Dragon." Throughout his childhood and teenage years in Hong Kong, Lee worked in approximately twenty Hong Kong movies.

In Hong Kong, the Lee family lived in a two-bedroom apartment in the Kowloon district. Bruce had two brothers and two sisters. His aunt and her five children also lived in the same house. This made for a very crowded household. Lee was known as a prankster, and with so many people living in the house, he probably had many opportunities to play jokes. Though Lee had a mischievous side to his personality, he also had a serious side and he always liked to read. When he was young, he had so much energy that his family called him "mo ti sing," which in English means "never sits still." Reading was one thing that could get Lee to sit still. As Lee grew up, he learned two languages. At home, his family spoke Cantonese, a dialect of Chinese. At La Salle Academy, where Lee went to school starting in 1952, he learned to speak English.

Hong Kong was a very rough place when Lee was growing up. As he got older, Lee started to get into many fights. Looking for a way to protect himself, Lee eventually turned to the martial arts. He began to study the Chinese martial art of kung fu, which is pronounced "gung fu" in Chinese. There are many types of kung fu, but Lee studied the style known as Wing Chun.

The Legend of Wing Chun

According to legend, Wing Chun was started over 300 years ago in southern China.

A young woman named Yim Wing Chun learned martial arts to protect herself from a bully who was trying to force her into marriage. After Yim Wing Chun practiced very hard, she mastered the techniques and challenged the bully to a fight. She beat him, and over time the style she mastered became known as Wing Chun.

The Young Martial Artist

Bruce Lee studied Wing Chun from a grandmaster named Yip Man. During this time, Lee learned the basics of how to punch, kick, and defend himself. He also became a very disciplined student, practicing Wing Chun between four and six hours every day.

In addition to the physical training, Lee also became interested in the philosophical aspects of the martial arts. From Yip Man, Lee learned about Eastern philosophy, such as the teachings of Buddha and Confucius. More important, he learned that studying the martial arts is more than just learning how to fight. When practiced properly, martial arts can also bring overall calmness and peace of mind. It is more than just learning how to punch and kick; it is a way of life meant to make the dedicated student a better person.

Though the philosophy behind Lee's Wing Chun training was instructing him to control his temper and stay away from fights, young Bruce just couldn't seem to do that.

Sifu Yip Man

Over the years, Wing Chun developed in China as it was passed down from one student to the next. Eventually, it was passed down to Grandmaster Yip Man. He brought Wing Chun from China to Hong Kong, where he became sifu (instructor) for many students, including Bruce Lee.

He continued to get into street fights. Eventually, Lee was expelled from La Salle Academy for fighting. At one point, his mother was brought into the police station to sign a paper promising that Bruce would stay out of trouble.

In 1959, when Lee was nineteen years old, his parents decided it was too risky for him to remain in Hong Kong. They couldn't stop him from getting into trouble, so they decided it was time for the son they had named "return again" to return to the place of his birth. It was time for Lee to make one of the biggest moves of his life. With a little over $100, Bruce Lee returned to San Francisco.

Chapter 2

Coming to America

When Bruce Lee arrived in San Francisco in 1959, he lived for a short time with a friend of his father. As a way to earn money, he gave dancing lessons. He stayed in San Francisco only for a short time before moving to Seattle. He lived with another one of his father's friends, a woman named Ruby Chow, who owned a restaurant. Lee worked in Ruby Chow's restaurant and lived in a small room above it. He also attended school in Seattle. Eventually, he earned a high school diploma, and then he enrolled at the University of Washington, where he studied philosophy. Lee's parents had sent him away from Hong Kong to keep him out of

The University of Washington circa 1961, when Bruce Lee was enrolled there

Cha-Cha Champion

Bruce Lee perfected his Wing Chun techniques through many hours of practice, but he also had time for other activities. One of his interests was cha-cha dancing. He worked hard to perfect his dance moves, and, at eighteen, he won a contest to become the cha-cha champion of Hong Kong.

Putting his championship skills to work, Lee gave dancing lessons to passengers aboard the steamship on his eighteen-day voyage from Hong Kong to San Francisco.

trouble, and it seemed like their plan worked perfectly.

In addition to working and going to school, Lee began to teach the martial arts. At first, he held small classes anywhere he could find space. Over time, Lee's reputation grew, and so did the number of his students. He became convinced that he could make a living teaching kung fu on a full-time basis. The students were impressed by Lee's incredible martial arts skills and by his magnetic personality, and they were also drawn to Lee because of his inspirational teaching style.

While at the University of Washington, Lee would often instruct his classes in secluded areas of the campus. Later, his kwoon (training hall) moved into a building near the university campus. He

Bruce Lee and his wife, Linda, attend the Stuntman's Annual Ball in Los Angeles, California, on November 26, 1966.

named his school the Jun Fan Gung Fu Institute. (Remember that Jun Fan was Lee's Chinese name.) One of the students attending Lee's classes while he was at the University of Washington was a young American woman named Linda Emery.

Fighting Tradition

Lee and Emery fell in love and were married in 1964. After the marriage, they moved to Oakland, California, where in the weeks before the wedding, Lee had started another school. As he continued to teach, he also learned more

Bruce Lee demonstrating a high kick in 1966

about the martial arts and developed his own beliefs about martial arts philosophy. At this point, Lee was a highly skilled martial artist, but he still wanted to be better.

Even though his training was based on kung fu, Lee blended techniques from other martial arts in order to make his fighting style more effective. This combination of styles would eventually lead Lee to develop his own martial arts philosophy, which he called jeet kune do ("the way of the intercepting fist").

Instead of sticking with a traditional system, Lee was designing a martial arts philosophy that was something new and modern. He was also doing something else that was quite different from the traditional martial arts schools. Lee's school was open to anyone who was serious

The Way of Jeet Kune Do

There are many different styles of martial arts. Some of the most familiar styles are karate, judo, tae kwon do, and kung fu.

Lee didn't refer to jeet kune do as a "style" because he wanted jeet kune do to be thought of as something completely different from the traditional styles. In jeet kune do, Lee blended modern fighting techniques with the most effective traditional martial arts.

about wanting to learn his art, regardless of their skin color or ethnic background.

In the United States today, there are thousands of martial arts schools. And, for the most part, these martial arts schools are open to anyone. This was not the case when Lee started teaching. At the time when he opened his kwoon, it was not generally acceptable to teach non-Asians. Traditional masters, especially the traditional kung fu instructors, viewed their martial art as a cultural property, and they did not want to share it with outsiders. They felt their secret fighting arts could be used against them.

With his exciting new brand of martial arts and his open-door policy, Lee was often seen in negative terms by many of the traditional instructors. Not only was he teaching something that he said was better than the traditional styles, he was also teaching martial arts to non-Asians. Many traditional martial arts masters were offended by Lee's modern policies. They were also jealous of him.

A martial arts enthusiast practices a move while reading Bruce Lee's book *Chinese Gung Fu: The Philosophical Art of Self-Defense*.

On one eventful day, a group of traditional masters issued a challenge to Bruce Lee. They picked a champion to fight against him. If Lee lost to their champion, he would have to close his school or stop teaching martial arts to non-Asian students.

Lee agreed to the challenge. The fight didn't last very long. Lee defeated his opponent very quickly. This battle was a very memorable occasion for Bruce Lee. On one hand, he was happy that he had won the fight and that he could continue to teach martial arts according to his own beliefs. On the other hand, Lee was not satisfied with his performance. He was unhappy that the fight had taken so long. Instead of minutes, he thought the fight should have been over in seconds. Also, although Lee was already in excellent physical condition, he became determined to be in perfect condition. He trained harder than ever before. His daily routine consisted of a highly demanding series of exercises and weight lifting. Lee began to think even more about his martial arts training and philosophy. Eventually, this challenge would turn out to be a major milestone for Bruce Lee's development of jeet kune do.

Hollywood Connections

Lee's reputation as a martial artist continued to grow. In 1964, at the First International Karate Championships in Long Beach, California, Lee demonstrated his famous "one-inch punch" and other extraordinary martial arts skills. There were some people in the audience who worked in

the entertainment industry, and as
a result of this demonstration, Lee
made contact with people who would
eventually help him start his career
in Hollywood.

The demonstration was filmed,
and Lee's explosive skills and
unique personality caught the eye of
a producer named William Dozier.

Dozier had a hit with the *Batman*
television series, and he was also
planning a new series called *Number
One Son* about a Chinese investigator.
Dozier was so impressed with Lee
that he wanted him to star in this
show. Lee was very excited by this
opportunity. Unfortunately, the series
was never made.

In 1965, the Lees' first child,
Brandon, was born. Like his father,
Brandon was born in the Chinese year
of the dragon. This was great news

for his parents. Unfortunately, at about the same time, bad news arrived from Hong Kong. One week after Brandon was born, Lee's father died, so Lee returned to Hong Kong for the funeral.

Even though *Number One Son* never became a television series, William Dozier remembered Lee, and it wasn't long before he came across a part that would be a perfect showcase for the explosive kicks and punches he'd first seen at the demonstration in Long Beach. In 1966, Lee got his first Hollywood break when Dozier cast him to play the part of Kato in *The Green Hornet*. Lee left the Oakland studio and moved his family to Los Angeles to start filming the television show.

Chapter 3

A Slow Road to Stardom

*T*he *Green Hornet* introduced
Bruce Lee to millions of
television viewers in America
and the rest of the world. In the show,
the Green Hornet was a newspaper
publisher with a secret identity as a
crime-fighting superhero. Lee played
Kato, the Green Hornet's chauffeur.
With an amazing display of martial
arts skills, Lee's Kato fought criminals
and used moves that had never been
seen before on television. In addition
to acting as Kato, Lee also

The Green Hornet (Van Williams) and Kato (Bruce Lee) are poised for action in the 1966 ABC television series *The Green Hornet*.

choreographed the fight scenes for *The Green Hornet*. One problem that he encountered during filming was that his moves were too fast for the cameras. The cameramen had to ask Lee to slow down so the camera could catch his movements.

Dressed in black and wearing a black eye mask and hat, Kato was a very exciting character. In fact, he was much more exciting than the Green Hornet. Lee's character didn't say much—he let fast and furious kicks and punches do all the talking.

In 1966, Lee made twenty-seven episodes of *The Green Hornet*. During that season, Lee became popular for his role as Kato. Unfortunately, the rest of the show didn't make such a splash. After only one season, *The Green Hornet* was canceled. Lee was very disappointed.

Kato Vs. The Boy Wonder

In an attempt to boost *The Green Hornet*'s popularity, the Green Hornet and Kato made an appearance on Batman. In the show, Kato fights Robin. After trading blows, the two eventually wind up in a tie. Unfortunately for Lee and the rest of *The Green Hornet* crew, the show's ratings did not turn around because of this appearance with the more popular dynamic duo.

Bruce Lee strikes three basic kung fu positions he used in the ABC-TV series *The Green Hornet* during a promotional event on November 30, 1966.

His first big Hollywood break had turned into a bust.

Although the series didn't last long, it would eventually help to propel Bruce Lee into super-stardom. In addition to introducing so many people to the martial arts, Lee proved that an Asian actor could become a popular television

Bruce Lee *(left)* and Van Williams, his co-star on *The Green Hornet,* practice a few kung fu moves.

star. Moreover, for Asians everywhere, Bruce Lee became a great source of pride because of his ability to break through racial barriers and become a Hollywood television star. He may have been the Green Hornet's sidekick, but for millions of fans, Bruce Lee was the true star of the show.

After The Green Hornet

After the cancellation of *The Green Hornet*, Lee found small parts in a few movies and television shows. He also worked as fight coordinator for a couple of movies. Even though Bruce was admired for his performance as Kato, he still couldn't find any Hollywood studios or producers willing to cast an Asian actor as the main star of a movie or television

Steve McQueen

Bruce Lee taught martial arts to a number of Hollywood celebrities. One of the most famous was charismatic tough-guy actor Steve McQueen.

McQueen was one of the biggest superstars at the time. His hit movies—none of which showcased his martial arts skills—include *The Great Escape, The Sand Pebbles, Bullitt,* and *Papillon.*

He was also one of Bruce Lee's good friends, although the relationship reportedly weakened when Lee's *Enter the Dragon* salary far exceeded McQueen's *Papillon* earnings. Still, McQueen served as a pallbearer at Lee's funeral.

series. He even appeared at a number of martial arts demonstrations throughout the country, and he continued teaching, opening a Jun Fan Gung Fu Institute in Los Angeles.

During this time, Lee taught private lessons to some of Hollywood's biggest stars. A few of his most famous students were the actors Steve McQueen and James Coburn and basketball superstar Kareem Abdul-Jabbar. As his reputation grew, Lee was able to charge as much as $275 an hour for private lessons. Even though Lee continued training as a martial artist, he still pursued the dream of getting steady acting work in Hollywood. He had tasted stardom thanks to his fame as Kato. Now, he looked for ways to build upon his reputation and become a major Hollywood star.

On April 19, 1969, Linda Lee gave birth to their second child, a daughter named Shannon Emery Lee. With a wife and two children to support, Bruce Lee continued to search for a steady acting job. One of his biggest career disappointments came during this time. In 1971, he began working with Warner Brothers to create a television series about a martial arts master in the American Old West. The proposed show was called *The Warrior*. As Lee developed the series and the character, he envisioned being the star.

However, the producers had different plans. They decided that they wanted someone less Asian-looking for the part, so they gave the role to an American actor named David Carradine. The television series was renamed *Kung Fu*, and it became a huge hit. Even though Carradine didn't know much about the martial arts, he became a major television star for his role as a kung fu master in the Wild West.

The Hollywood system had turned its back on Bruce Lee. As an actor and martial artist, Lee was more qualified than anyone to play the part. Yet, the producers weren't brave enough to take a chance on an Asian actor. Once again, Bruce Lee was left to wonder what it would take for him to become a star in America.

Overcoming Injury

In addition to his frustrations and disappointments as an actor, Lee faced an even bigger battle in 1970. During weight-lifting training, Lee suffered a very serious back injury. The injury was so severe that doctors told Lee he'd never be able to perform martial arts in the same way again. Bruce Lee was someone who truly believed in hard work and the power of positive thinking. He maintained a positive outlook and refused to give up.

During months of recovery, Lee rested and then slowly began to practice martial arts again. Though he would never be completely pain-free from this serious injury, Lee was eventually able to train just as hard as before.

In terms of the development of jeet kune do, something positive came out of this injury. While Lee's bad back was healing, he continued to develop his theories about the martial arts. As he'd learned years earlier from Yip Man, Lee showed that his martial art was not just about physical training. During this time, he spent much time studying and writing down his philosophy of jeet kune do. The notes he took during this time became the basis for his book, *Tao of Jeet Kune Do*, which was published after his death.

In 1971, Lee traveled to Hong Kong to visit his mother. He didn't know it at the time, but this trip would change his life once again. After struggling in vain to achieve acting success in America, he unexpectedly found stardom in Asia. Though *The Green Hornet* had been canceled in the United States after one season, it had become one of the most popular television shows in Hong Kong. When Lee returned to Hong Kong, he discovered that he was a star.

Chapter 4

The Big Screen

When Bruce Lee was growing up in Hong Kong, he had appeared in many movies. He even became somewhat popular for these roles. In his last role before moving to the United States, he starred as a troubled teenager in a movie called *The Orphan*. But nothing compared with the fame he achieved from *The Green Hornet*. From the moment he stepped off the airplane, Lee was a star.

Lee was so popular in Hong Kong that *The Green Hornet* was called *The Kato Show*, and there was no doubt about who the main star was. In little time, Lee started to receive offers to be in Hong Kong martial arts movies. He also appeared on Hong Kong television talk shows to discuss his career and to demonstrate his spectacular martial arts skills. After struggling for so many years to land a steady job in Hollywood, Lee came home to Hong Kong as a celebrity. With movie offers coming his way, Lee decided to continue his acting career in Hong Kong.

In July 1971, Lee started filming *The Big Boss* in a small village in Thailand. (The movie would be released in the United States as *Fists of Fury*.) It was a small-budget

KARATE KUNG-FU!

The oriental sensation— now gives America the action its been waiting for!

Bruce Lee

every limb of his body is a lethal weapon in

"Fists of Fury"

National General Pictures presents Bruce Lee in "FISTS OF FURY" • Produced by Raymond Chow
Screenplay and Direction by Lo Wei • Color • A National General Pictures Release

73/117

With his innovative martial arts maneuvers, Bruce Lee offered a refreshing twist for American action movie fans in *Fists of Fury.*

movie, and the conditions on the film set were not very good. The weather was bad, the food was poor, and the production was disorganized. Like many martial arts movies, the plot of *The Big Boss* was very predictable: Lee plays the part of a young man

Cheng Chao-an (Bruce Lee) shows a bad guy who's boss with a powerful punch in *The Big Boss.*

from the country who comes to the city to work. He finds a job at an ice factory where some of his family and friends also work. As it turns out, gangsters also use the factory as a base for their drug-smuggling operations. When he had left the country, Lee's character (Chen Chao-an) had made a pledge to his mother that he wouldn't ever fight again. He does his best to stay out of trouble, but after a while the gangsters push him too far. He is forced to defend his family and himself. When Cheng gets going, the gangsters are sorry they ever messed with him. In one incredible fight scene, Lee's character single-handedly defeats a bunch of bad guys at the ice factory. They attack him with punches and kicks, knives and clubs, chains and ice picks, but they can't match his unleashed fury.

The making of the movie was not an enjoyable experience for Lee, particularly since he missed his family very much. In the end, though, things worked out perfectly. The movie was a smash hit. In October 1971, Linda came to Hong Kong for the premiere of *The Big Boss*. As they watched the movie, the Lees wondered if the audience would like it or not. They had nothing to worry about. When the movie ended, the audience cheered wildly for their new martial arts hero. Soon *The Big Boss* would become the best-selling movie in Hong Kong and a huge hit throughout Southeast Asia.

Making a Statement

Even though the story and the characters were nothing out of the ordinary compared to other martial arts films at the time, the action in *The Big Boss* was something very special. Lee's punches and kicks seemed to explode on the screen. He was more powerful and faster than anyone the audience had seen before. Plus, Lee had an electric screen

Bruce Lee had an electrifying screen presence—it was like nothing seen before or since.

presence to go along with his great skills. Movie audiences in Hong Kong and throughout Southeast Asia were amazed at what Lee could do. It was almost like seeing an incredible magician at work. They could watch him, but the speed and power of his kicks and punches were such that

Bruce Lee had many ways to take care of an attacker, as he demonstrates in this scene from *Fist of Fury* (released in the United States as *The Chinese Connection*).

audiences couldn't believe what they were seeing. Now that Lee was so popular, the Hong Kong audience had higher expectations, and Lee didn't let them down. His next film was called *Fist of Fury* (released in America as *The Chinese Connection*).

In this movie, Lee plays the part of a Chinese martial arts student. As in his first movie, his character had made a promise not to fight. So, when a group of Japanese martial artists challenges his school, he can't do anything about it. The Japanese students insult the Chinese students, forcing them to carry a sign that reads "The Chinese are the sick men of Asia." As in *The Big Boss*, Lee's character holds back. He doesn't want to break his promise. Later, though, he pays a visit to the Japanese school, where he replies to

Lee's kicks were fast and powerful, as he shows in this scene from *Fist of Fury*.

their insults in the only way he knows how. In a spectacular scene, Bruce's character defeats the entire Japanese school. He lets them know that "the Chinese are not the sick men of Asia."

Fist of Fury became even more successful than the record-setting *The Big Boss*. And, with the success, Lee became even more popular throughout Asia. In Hong Kong, he couldn't even go out of his house without fans mobbing him for autographs. Some fans wanted more than an autograph. On numerous occasions, challengers approached Lee looking for a fight. They wanted to see if his martial arts skills were real, or just something that looked good on the big screen. Mostly, Lee ignored these challengers, but there were times when he was forced to fight. Like the bad guys in his movies, these challengers would ultimately learn that it wasn't a good idea to make Bruce Lee angry.

Total Control

With two very successful movies under his belt, Bruce Lee wanted to do something bigger and better for his next project. Now that he was able to demand more money and more control over his movies, Lee was convinced he could make a higher quality movie than the two previous pictures. In 1972, he began work on *The Way of the Dragon*. (This movie would later be released in the United States as *Return of the Dragon* because it came out after *Enter the Dragon*.) In addition to starring in this movie, Lee wrote it,

With an intense look and a loud yell, Bruce Lee takes care of an attacker in *The Way of the Dragon*.

produced it, and directed it. In an attempt to draw more of an international audience, he made the extraordinary move of filming the movie in Italy. It was the first time a Hong Kong film was made in Europe. He also cast many non-Asian actors, including an American karate champion named Chuck Norris.

The movie's theme is the struggle of good against evil. Lee plays the good Tang Lung, who has traveled to Rome from Hong Kong to help defend his family's restaurant against a gang. Throughout the movie, Tang Lung defeats the gangsters and warns them to stay away from the restaurant. Finally, the gang boss decides to hire an expert martial arts hit man to take Tang Lung down. Chuck Norris plays Colt, hired by the evil boss to eliminate Tang Lung.

In the film's climactic scene, Tang Lung battles head-to-head against Colt. The fight takes place in Rome's Colosseum, a fitting setting for this battle between two martial arts warriors. Like two gladiators from ancient Rome, Tang Lung and Colt battle to the death. It's one of

Tang Lung (Bruce Lee) and Colt (Chuck Norris) square off in a climactic scene from *Return of the Dragon*.

the classic martial arts movie scenes of all time. No one else appears in the scene as they prepare to fight. Only a scrawny kitten looks on, the lone spectator of this battle of martial arts titans. When the kitten suddenly hisses, the fighters attack each other. At first, Lee's character seems surprised by the speed of the American assassin. And, as the little kitten looks on, Colt quickly gets the better of Tang Lung. Eventually, though, Tang Lung changes his tactics, using his quickness and his catlike agility to move away from Colt. As Colt becomes frustrated, Tang Lung sees his chance to move. With a series of awesome punches and spinning kicks, Tang Lung turns the tide of the fight. In the end, only one gladiator remains standing.

Chuck Norris

Before costarring in *The Way of the Dragon*, Chuck Norris had trained with Bruce Lee. Millions of fans now know Norris for his role in *Walker, Texas Ranger* and for many other action movies. At the time he made *The Way of the Dragon*, Norris was an accomplished American karate champion, but he was unknown as an actor.

Legend has it that, once Norris arrived on the *Dragon* set ready to face off with his friend and training partner, the film's producers realized that the two actors were nearly identical in size. Since they wanted Norris to outweigh Lee, they ordered him to gain twenty pounds fast. A diet of hamburgers and malts and the elimination of workouts bulked up Norris. He claims, however, that he was all fat and no muscle, which is why you don't see him performing jumping kicks— with all the extra weight, he couldn't get off the ground!

The Way of Bruce Lee

As Bruce Lee took more control of his movies, he was able to incorporate some of his martial arts philosophy into the scripts. In *The Way of the Dragon*, for instance, Lee's Tang Lung makes a comment about how it doesn't matter where your moves come from; it's more important that the techniques work. In other words, if something works for you, use it and don't worry about the origin of the technique.

Later, in the fight with Norris's Colt, Lee's Tang Lung is on the verge of losing the fight. In order to win, he has to change his strategy. He realizes in midfight that the style of fighting he's using is not working, so he makes a quick change to take advantage of his superior speed and agility. Because of his ability to adapt and outsmart his opponent, Tang Lung is able to win. These concepts are a large part of the philosophy behind jeet kune do.

For *The Way of the Dragon*, Lee had taken on more responsibility and more work. It paid off. Like his previous movies, this one became an immediate success throughout Asia. It would have been easy for Lee to keep making Hong Kong movies and ride on this growing wave of success. However, he was now in a position to take on a greater challenge. He was ready once again to face one opponent that he'd yet to conquer. He was ready once again to take on Hollywood.

Chapter 5

Birth of a Legend

After he finished *The Way of the Dragon*, Lee began working on a movie called *The Game of Death*. While filming fight scenes for this movie, he was drawn away to fulfill a dream he'd been pursuing for a long time. Finally, he was offered a Hollywood movie deal. This new project would be coproduced by Warner Brothers and would have an American director and an international cast.

Finally, Bruce Lee would get the chance to star in a Hollywood movie and prove the industry wrong in its thinking that an Asian actor couldn't be a major star.

The movie was *Enter the Dragon*. Even now, more than several decades after its release,

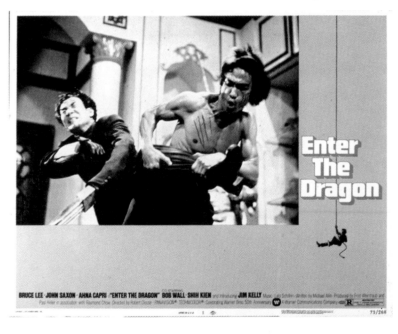

Over the years, *Enter the Dragon* has become the martial arts movie against which all others are judged.

Enter the Dragon is still considered by many to be the greatest martial arts movie of all time. Many action stars have followed in Bruce Lee's powerful footsteps, but none have made a martial arts movie so universally admired as *Enter the Dragon*.

In *Enter the Dragon*, Bruce Lee plays the part of Lee, a master martial artist sent to a mysterious island owned by Mr. Han (played by Shih Kien). The island serves as a base for Han's massive drug manufacturing operations. Every three years, Han hosts a martial arts tournament pitting the best fighters against each other. He also uses the tournament to recruit the most lethal talent to join his criminal activities. Lee's mission is to go undercover to the tournament, using his invitation as a means of destroying Han's evil empire. As extra

Jackie Chan

Today, Jackie Chan is one of the biggest movie stars in the world. Early in his career, he had a short on-screen meeting with Bruce Lee. Watch very closely to see Jackie in *Enter the Dragon*. In an exciting fight scene in the tunnels under Han's island, Bruce takes out a lot of bad guys. One of them is Jackie Chan.

Following Lee's death, action film producers scrambled to find the next Bruce Lee. Jackie Chan was cast as Lee's replacement in a remake of *Fist of Fury*. But Chan could not be Bruce Lee, and he desperately wanted to showcase his own style as an action hero. After years of frustration and box office disappointments, Chan was finally allowed to perform as Jackie Chan—a martial arts hero with a slapstick sense of humor. With hits like *Rush Hour* and *Rush Hour II*, *Drunken Master*, *Shanghai Noon*, and *Rumble in the Bronx*, Chan has found his own place in action film history.

motivation, Lee learns that Han's main man, a brutal killer named Oharra (played by Bob Wall), was the person responsible for the death of Lee's sister. From the beginning, this character is much different than the people Lee played in his previous movies. Instead of a simple country bumpkin, Lee in *Enter the Dragon* is more like a James Bond type of secret agent. He's smart and sophisticated, and, of course, extremely lethal.

During the day, Lee participates in Han's tournament, where he displays his impressive skills and watches the other expert martial artists at work. At night, Lee explores the dark side of Han's island. In a series of tunnels beneath the island, he discovers the drug manufacturing plant as well as a prison holding many down-and-out Chinese men. After exacting revenge

Lee gets creative during the fight against Oharra in *Enter the Dragon*.

on Oharra in a spectacular, emotion-filled fight, Lee sets his sights on disrupting Han's illegal activities once and for all.

In the climactic fight scene, Lee battles Han face-to-face. Like Lee, Han is a superior martial artist. But Han also has a devious and lethal secret weapon. Some time in his past, Han had lost a hand. Now he is able to fit his arm with one of a number of diabolical attachments, such as a solid metal skeletal hand, a bear claw, and a four-pronged knife. He's a ruthless and cunning opponent with excellent skills and a lethal hidden weapon—the perfect foe for Bruce Lee.

The final fight starts amid a battle between hundreds of Han's men fighting against the escaping prisoners. When the brawl starts, Han runs for the safety of his palace. Lee follows. As in the climactic fight with Chuck Norris in *The Way of the Dragon*, this fight becomes an epic one-on-one battle to the death. Eventually, the fighters wind up in a room full of mirrors. Han has the advantage because he knows the room. At first, Lee seems confused, not knowing if he's looking at the real Han or at Han's reflection. Meanwhile, Han stays hidden, lashing out every so often with his razor-sharp knife-hand. In the end, Lee smashes all the mirrors and exposes the evil Han. With a powerful sidekick, Lee ends the battle and puts an end to Han's evil island.

Troubled Times

In spite of Bruce Lee's success, he faced a number of problems while

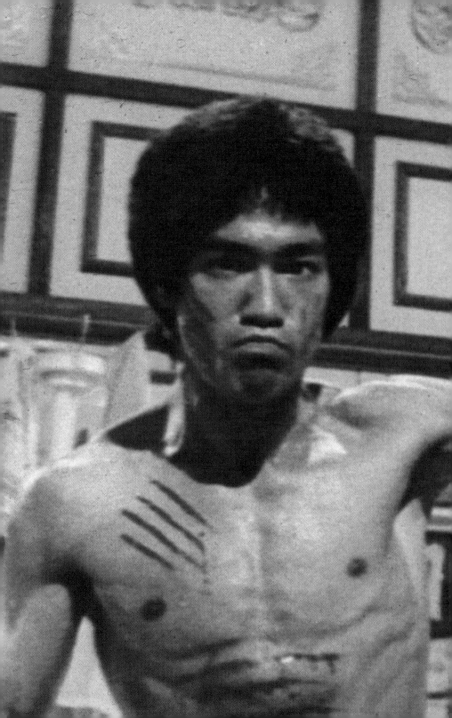

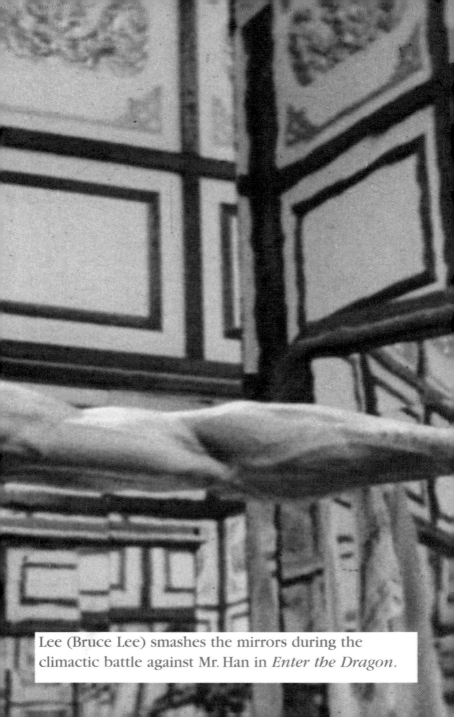

Lee (Bruce Lee) smashes the mirrors during the climactic battle against Mr. Han in *Enter the Dragon*.

Bruce Lee and producer Fred Weintraub discuss a scene during the production of *Enter the Dragon* in Hong Kong.

making *Enter the Dragon*. Some of the problems included cultural obstacles stemming from the fact that half the film crew was from America and they weren't used to the conditions in Hong Kong. There were also problems with the script, and at one point Lee threatened to quit because of disagreements with the screenwriter. Additional problems included a threatened strike by the extras and the usual problem of people wanting to challenge Lee to a fight.

On top of everything else, there were a number of injuries on the set. In one instance, when Lee was filming the fight scene against Oharra, the defeated Oharra tries one last desperate attempt to hurt Lee with two broken bottles. During the filming, the timing of the actors was not quite right, and Bruce severely cut his hand. The wound required many stitches, and filming was postponed for a number of days. In spite of these difficulties, the crew finished filming. Unfortunately, the worst trouble was yet to come.

After the filming was complete, Lee was working on the sound for

Enter the Dragon. On July 20, 1973, he suddenly felt faint and collapsed. He was rushed to the hospital, where Linda joined him. It was a real scare for everyone. Doctors examined him and prescribed medication for swelling of the brain. Though it was viewed as a serious health problem, Lee seemed to recover fully. In order to get a second opinion, he traveled to the United States for an examination by a specialist. He was given a clean bill of health and returned to Hong Kong to prepare for the release of *Enter the Dragon.*

Then the unthinkable occurred. Just a few short months after his first collapse, Lee was meeting with film producer Raymond Chow and actress Betty Ting Pei to talk about the script for *The Game of Death.*

Complaining of a bad headache, Lee took some prescription medicine that the actress had given him and then he fell asleep. This time he didn't wake up. As with his previous collapse, Lee was rushed to the hospital. This time, though, he would not recover. The dragon was dead.

Chapter 6

Long Live The Dragon

It was unbelievable to think that the mighty dragon was dead at the young age of thirty-two. When you see him in *Enter the Dragon*, you see Bruce Lee at the peak of physical fitness. How could it be, then, that he wouldn't live to see the release of the movie that would catapult him to international superstardom?

When Lee died, there was much speculation and many rumors about why he died. There was gossip that traditional martial artists, displeased at the arrogance and success of this young star, had killed him with some sort of curse or secret martial arts death technique. There were rumors that Chinese gangsters had killed him because he wouldn't agree to work with them. It was even rumored that he wasn't dead and that the story of his death was made up as a publicity stunt for the release of *Enter the Dragon*. People just couldn't accept the fact that this screen hero was gone.

All sorts of other wild stories came out after his death, but the only thing that really mattered was that Lee was gone. According to the doctors who examined his body, Bruce Lee had died because of a swelling of the brain caused by a

Bruce Lee's death came as a shock to his millions of fans around the world. It was impossible to believe that their hero was gone.

rare allergic reaction to the medicine he took on the night he died.

There were two funeral ceremonies for Lee. The first funeral was in Hong Kong, where thousands of fans jammed the streets to join family and friends mourning the loss of their hero. In a smaller service in Seattle, Lee was laid to rest. Within a few short weeks of his death, *Enter the Dragon* was released. Its premiere in the United States was at the famous Grauman's Chinese Theatre in Hollywood. Finally, Bruce Lee proved to Hollywood and the rest of the world that he could be a bigger star than anyone would ever have imagined.

In 1978, *The Game of Death* was released. The movie includes scenes that Lee completed before his death.

Although Bruce Lee was unable to complete *The Game of Death*, he did film some great fight scenes for the movie that was pieced together after his death.

Kareem Abdul-Jabbar

Kareem Abdul-Jabbar is best known for his lengthy basketball career. But the Hall of Famer also trained with Bruce Lee in Los Angeles. In the climactic scene of *The Game of Death*, Lee and Abdul-Jabbar square off in a battle of contrasting styles and sizes. With almost a 2-foot height advantage, Abdul-Jabbar was a fascinating opponent for Lee.

The rest of the movie features an actor filling in for Lee's part. Lee's fight scenes at the end of the movie offer further proof of his great skills.

Lasting Appeal

Throughout his career as a martial artist and as an action movie star, Bruce Lee faced many obstacles in both his personal and professional lives. Though he experienced many disappointments, Bruce Lee continued to maintain a positive outlook and always worked very hard to reach his goals. His life was short, but it inspired many others, and it continues to do so to this day. Even now, many years after his death, Bruce Lee's status as an international martial arts legend and action movie star continues to

Shannon Lee *(left)*, Bruce Lee's daughter, and Linda Lee Cadwell, Bruce Lee's wife, pose next to a photo panel of the martial arts legend at the opening of an exhibition in Tokyo, Japan, on August 3, 1998.

grow. Because Bruce Lee broke down so many barriers, he was able to pave the road for the tremendous success that the martial arts have today.

In recent times, Asian movies have hit a mainstream international audience like never before. Nothing better symbolizes this breakthrough than director Ang Lee's *Crouching Tiger, Hidden Dragon*, which was nominated for ten Academy Awards in 2001, including best picture.

It has been many years since Bruce Lee's death, but his lasting appeal lives on. The impact he made on action movies and on the martial arts in general continues to grow. For those interested in studying his martial art of jeet kune do, it continues to thrive under the leadership of his former students

Son of the Dragon

Brandon Lee followed in his father's footsteps by becoming an actor. Unfortunately, like his father, Brandon Lee did not live to see the release of his biggest film. Brandon was tragically killed on the set while filming *The Crow*. Only twenty-eight years old, Brandon Lee was buried next to his father at a cemetery in Seattle.

and other followers. For more advanced martial arts students, Lee's words live on in the books published after his death, including *Tao of Jeet Kune Do*. His life and teachings continue to be the subject of many books, magazines, and films, and there are countless fan sites on the Internet devoted to him.

In 1992, Lee's life story served as the basis for a major Hollywood motion picture (*Dragon: The Bruce Lee Story*). In 1998, Warner Brothers released a 25th anniversary special edition of *Enter the Dragon* with footage that had been cut from the original American release. In 2000, the Chinese Cultural Center in San Francisco's Chinatown district paid tribute to Bruce Lee with an exhibition of approximately 250 items related to Lee's life and movies.

Tamy Kimura, who was Bruce Lee's assistant instructor, visits the martial arts legend's grave in Seattle, Washington.

It's obvious that Lee lives on in so many ways. Most important, for martial artists, action movie fans, and anyone interested in glimpsing one of the most powerful and inspirational stars ever to hit the big screen, Bruce Lee's movies remain an explosive testament to his everlasting skill and charisma.

Filmography

Film Appearances

The Orphan (1960)

Marlowe (1969)

The Big Boss (1971)
Released as *Fists of Fury*
in the United States

Fist of Fury (1972)
Released as *The Chinese Connection*
in the United States

The Way of the Dragon (1973)
Released as *Return of the Dragon*
in the United States

Enter the Dragon (1973)

The Game of Death
(completed in 1978)

Television Appearances

The Green Hornet (1966) as "Kato"

Batman (1966) as "Kato"

Longstreet (1971) as "Li Tsung"

Glossary

gung fu An ancient Chinese martial art form. It is also known as kung fu.

jeet kune do The martial art developed by Bruce Lee, which translates as "the way of the intercepting fist."

karate A Japanese martial art.

Kato In the television show *The Green Hornet*, Bruce Lee played the role of Kato, a high-kicking chauffeur for the crime-fighting Green Hornet.

kwoon The Chinese term for training hall.

martial artist A practitioner of the martial arts.

martial arts A formalized fighting and self-defense system that becomes a way of life.

sifu The Chinese word for teacher.

Wing Chun An ancient branch of gung fu that, according to legend, was developed by a woman named Yim Wing Chun to protect herself from a bully.

For More Information

American Academy for Korean Martial
   Instruction
29 North Cass Avenue
Westmont, IL 60559
(630) 852-4422
e-mail: info@americanmartialarts.net
Web site: http://www.americanmartialarts.net

Bruce Lee Educational Foundation
P.O. Box 1390
Clovis, CA 93613-1390
Web site: http://www.jkd.com

Martialinfo.com
P.O. Box 10911
Canoga Park, CA 91309
e-mail: mi_info@pacbell.net
Web site: http://www.martialinfo.com

Web Sites

http://www.brucelee.com

http://www.brucelee.org.uk

For Further Reading

Lee, Bruce. *The Celebrated Life of the Golden Dragon*. Edited by John Little. North Clarendon, VT: Tuttle Publishing, 2000.

Lee, Bruce. *Tao of Jeet Kune Do*. Santa Clarita, CA: Ohara Publications, Inc., 1975.

Lee, Linda. *The Bruce Lee Story*. Santa Clarita, CA: Ohara Publications, Inc., 1989.

Lewis, Jon E. Bruce Lee. Philadelphia: Chelsea House Publishers, 1998.

Metil, Luana, and Jace Townsend. *The Story of Karate: From Buddhism to Bruce Lee*. Minneapolis: Lerner Publications Company, 1995.

Tagliaferro, Linda. *Bruce Lee*. Minneapolis: Lerner Publications Company, 2000.

Index

109

About the Author

Greg Roensch is a writer who lives in San Francisco, California. He also works as managing editor for a video-game publisher.

Acknowledgments

My deepest appreciation goes to Master Larry E. Walker. Special thanks also to Kent Kitagawa and the students at KIK's Tae Kwon Do.

Photo Credits

Cover, pp. 70, 90–91, 96, 100 © AP/Wide World Photos; pp. 4, 30, 40, 42, 44–45, 55, 56, 59, 60, 62–63, 66, 68–69, 75, 79, 82–83, 84, 93, 94, 98 © Everett Collection; p. 7 © AFP/Corbis; pp. 8, 17, 28–29 © Hulton/Archive; p. 25 © MSCUA, University of Washington Libraries, UW17622; p. 34 photo by Cindy Reiman; p. 43 © Bettmann/Corbis.

Series Design and Layout

Les Kanturek